Animals and Their Niches

HOW SPECIES SHARE RESOURCES

Laurence Pringle
illustrated by Leslie Morrill

William Morrow and Company
New York 1977

Text copyright © 1977 by Laurence Pringle
Illustrations copyright © 1977 by Leslie Morrill
All rights reserved. No part of this book may be reproduced or utilized in any form or by any means, electronic or mechanical, including photocopying, recording or by any information storage and retrieval system, without permission in writing from the Publisher. Inquiries should be addressed to William Morrow and Company, Inc., 105 Madison Ave., New York, N.Y. 10016. Printed in the United States of America.

1 2 3 4 5 6 7 8 9 10

Library of Congress Cataloging in Publication Data

Pringle, Laurence P.   Animals and their niches.
Bibliography: pp. 61–62.
Summary: Discusses the sharing of food and other resources among species of animals that live in the same community.
1. Biotic communities—Juvenile literature. 2. Ecology—Juvenile literature. [1. Biotic communities. 2. Ecology]
I. Morrill, Leslie. II. Title. QH541.14.P73   591.5   77-3636
ISBN 0-688-22127-0
ISBN 0-688-32127-5 lib. bdg.

The author wishes to thank Dr. Robert Leo Smith, Division of Forestry, West Virginia University, for reading the manuscript of this book and suggesting changes in it.

Contents

Survival and Sharing 5
Three Kinds of Garter Snakes 15
Evergreen Warblers 22
The Minnows of Long Lake 30
Desert Rodents 41
Understanding Niches 50
Glossary 59
Further Reading 61
Index 63

Survival and Sharing

The earth is only a small planet, but it is rich in life. There are about 4,500 species of mammals, 6,000 reptiles, 8,600 birds, and 20,000 fishes. Biologists estimate that there are 900,000 kinds of insects known so far, with many more yet to be discovered and named.

Giving names to animals and plants is important, but it is only the first step toward understanding life on our planet. There is much more to learn. Have you ever wondered why there are so many different kinds of animals? And how one kind of animal affects other kinds?

The questions seem simple, but the answers are complicated and far from complete. This book is about one such "simple" question that biologists wonder about: How are food and other resources shared among species that live in the same place?

As you probably know, animals and plants live together in groupings. A pond has one group, a forest another. Together these populations of animals and plants are called "communities." A community is a system, or network, of animal and plant populations that live together in a specific place. It is like a community of people in many ways.

In plant-animal communities each kind of organism has a job or role called its "niche." Our usual idea of a job is that of a teacher, nurse, or carpenter. But niche is more complex. In fact, ecologists have not yet agreed on a precise definition for this term. However, many would probably

---

Life is especially abundant
where a land community and a water community meet.

agree that a niche is the total of an organism's relationships with other living and nonliving things in its community. (We think of niches mainly for populations and species of organisms, but each individual has its own niche too.)

It is probably impossible to know everything about an animal's niche, since it is so much more complex than a job. In a human community, for example, one person's job may be a teacher but his or her niche might include being a parent, a voter, a consumer of certain kinds and amounts of food, and much more. In a wild community, part of a mouse's niche may be to eat seeds of a certain kind and size, to produce young at a particular season, to be active at certain times of the day in certain places, and even to be *eaten* by a fox or an owl.

Part of an owl's niche is to eat mice.
And a mouse's niche includes
the possibility of being eaten by an owl.

Usually an animal must get its food and everything else it needs for life from its community. In each community, however, there is only a certain amount of food, water, space, and other resources. Suppose that two different kinds of birds both eat the same small insects. Can they coexist, or does one bird population die out?

Biologists have thought about this matter for a long time. More than a century ago, biologist Charles Darwin wrote about this competition among animals in his classic work, *The Origin of Species*. In 1904, an ornithologist named Joseph Grinnell wrote, "Two species of approximately the same food habits are not likely to remain long enough evenly balanced in numbers in the same region. One will crowd out the other."

During the 1920s two mathematicians, each unaware of the other's work, studied the "struggle for existence" among species.

They developed formulas that showed how one species would win out over another if both competed for the same food or resource.

Russian biologist B.F. Gause decided to investigate this idea in a laboratory. In a flask he put water and a supply of food (bacteria). Then he added a few individuals of two kinds of tiny animals known as parameciums. At first both kinds increased rapidly. In about three weeks, however, one species had died out. The other kind of paramecium succeeded because it was able to reproduce faster.

Later Gause matched another species of paramecium against the kind that had died out in the earlier experiment. This time both species survived. Why? One kind fed on bacteria that settled on the bottom of the flask. The other kind ate bacteria in the open water. Even though they both ate the only food available in their community, they fed in different

11

places. They had different niches, so there was little direct competition for the food.

Other biologists also investigated how animals compete for resources. In England, A.C. Crombie put equal numbers of two beetle species in a container with their food: flour. One species died out, mostly because many of its eggs were eaten by its competitor. In another experiment, two species of grain beetles were put in a container that held some cracked wheat. This time both species survived. They both ate the wheat, but one species lived among the grains while the other lived and fed on the outer surface of the grains. They both shared the same resource, but each used a part the other could not reach.

The results of these and other laboratory studies suggested a possible rule, or principle, of nature: *complete competitors cannot coexist.* If they need exactly the same

---

grain beetles and their larvae

foods and resources, only one competitor will survive. If they do coexist, this means that they *must* differ in some ways—perhaps in the kind or size of food they eat, or the time of day they are active. These differences allow animals to use resources unavailable to others. Of course they do not share resources in the same way you might give a friend half of your candy bar. The ways animals share have evolved over thousands and perhaps millions of years.

The idea that animals somehow share resources has fascinated many biologists. But this competition principle was based on only a few observations in simple laboratory experiments. Scientists wondered what they might discover by studying real communities of plants and animals in nature.

Three Kinds of Garter Snakes

Hundreds of species of animals may live together in a community. It is plain to see that many of them have different needs. A seed-eating bird does not compete for food with a bird that eats insects. However, in the late 1940s a biologist named Charles Carpenter puzzled over how three different kinds of garter snakes all lived together in the same forty-eight-acre area near Ann Arbor, Michigan. The snakes, Butler's garter snake, the ribbon snake, and the common garter snake, were closely related and about the same size. How did they coexist?

To find out, Charles Carpenter spent

three years walking back and forth over the study area. It was made up of several habitats, or living places—marsh, pasture, forest, a creek, and some small ponds. He poked into clumps of grass and pried into bushes and thickets. He became adept at catching snakes, capturing more than 2,000 (some individuals caught more than once). He noted the location of each capture on a map of the area. And each snake caught for the first time was marked so that it could be recognized if caught again.

Before releasing a snake, Carpenter squeezed its abdomen in a way that caused the animal to regurgitate whatever food it contained. Most of the time he could identify what the snake had eaten. Usually the food was only partly digested; sometimes it was still alive!

Carpenter discovered that Butler's garter

a garter snake

snake fed on earthworms and leeches. The common garter snake also ate many earthworms, but ate tadpoles, frogs, caterpillars, and a few mice and small birds too. The ribbon snake fed almost entirely on tadpoles, frogs, and fish.

At the beginning of his study, Carpenter noticed no difference in the habitat of the snakes. However, whenever he caught a snake he made notes about its surroundings. In winter he found that all three species hibernated on the same south-facing hillside. In the spring the snakes emerged from their dens at different times, and they were usually found in different habitats during the summer.

Butler's garter snakes lived among the dense grasses near water. They were never seen in the forest. Ribbon snakes were also found near water, but were most abundant in bushy areas. In fact, many of the

a ribbon snake swallowing a leopard frog

ribbon snakes Carpenter saw had climbed several feet up into bushes. The common garter snakes lived in a variety of habitats.

Carpenter often found individuals of the three species close together, sometimes within inches of one another. Nevertheless, his observations of the snakes' habitat and foods showed that the populations had different niches. They seemed to coexist with very little competition.

Charles Carpenter often found ribbon snakes in bushes.

Evergreen Warblers

A few years after Carpenter's study, a biologist named Robert MacArthur began an especially important study of how animals share resources. His observations were made in the evergreen forests of Vermont and Maine, where five species of warblers lived in summer. The warblers all ate insects, which they caught in spruce and fir trees. And they all nested in the same kinds of trees. How did the warblers coexist?

left: Blackburnian warblers search for insects on branches. right: Cape May warblers often dart after flying insects. Most North American warblers are about four and a half inches long.

Robert MacArthur spent hundreds of hours watching warblers as they searched for food. Early in his investigation he noticed that the birds had different ways of hunting and also fed in different parts, or zones, of the trees.

The Cape May warbler fed near the tops of trees and among the outer part of top branches. There it hawked, or darted, after flying insects. In contrast, the Blackburnian warbler seldom hawked. It did feed near the treetops, but explored limbs from their bases at the tree trunk out to their tips.

In the middle zones of trees MacArthur saw the black-throated green warbler, hopping about on the dense mats of evergreen needles. It looked for insects among the needles underfoot. It also peered up into branches overhead. If it saw insects there, this warbler hovered in the air and plucked them off.

Another species, the bay-breasted warbler, fed in the middle and lower zones of the evergreens. It rarely hovered. It explored branches from their bases to their tips, staying mostly near the interior of a tree. This species moved much more slowly than the others and stayed in one tree for a long time.

The fifth species MacArthur observed had the most varied feeding pattern. Sometimes he saw the myrtle warbler in thick foliage near treetops. Sometimes it fed among the lowest branches and on the ground beneath trees. It moved up, down, and sideways on branches. It hawked after flying prey. And it moved rather quickly from one tree to another, searching them less thoroughly than the other four species.

MacArthur wondered whether the warblers also differed in the kinds of food they sought. He measured the bills of the five species. They were quite close in size, so the warblers probably caught animals of a similar size. From this evidence and from

the results of some studies of the contents of warbler stomachs, MacArthur concluded that the warblers ate whatever kinds of insects and spiders they found. Any difference in their food could be explained by the differences in their feeding zones. For example, Blackburnian warblers might eat more beetles than the other warblers because they hunted where beetles were most likely to live—on or near tree trunks, not at the tips of branches.

Since MacArthur watched warblers in the summertime, he saw the birds nesting and raising young. He also learned about their breeding from the studies of other biologists. All of these observations showed that the warblers usually built their nests in their preferred feeding zones. There were also differences in the periods during

above: Bay-breasted warblers move more slowly than most warblers.
below: Myrtle warblers sometimes hunt for insects near or on the ground.

27

which the warblers raised their young—a time when parent birds need to gather much more food than usual. So the warblers' greatest need for food came at different times during the summer.

There was some overlap in nesting times. And, of course, individual warblers sometimes fed beyond the zones that were preferred by their species. Nevertheless, Robert MacArthur's research showed that five kinds of closely related animals could coexist while they all sought the same kinds of food at the same time and even in the same trees.

a male black-throated green warbler feeding its young

The Minnows of Long Lake

During the 1960s and 1970s, the study of animal niches became very popular among biologists. They were fascinated by the variety of ways in which animal niches differed, permitting a sharing of resources. This sharing was often called "resource partitioning."

Land animals, including ants and chipmunks, were most often the subject of research. They are usually much easier to observe than water animals. However, one of the most detailed studies of animal niches was made of minnows in a Minnesota lake.

In the summer of 1966, Peter Moyle

began netting samples of minnow populations from shallow waters at both ends of Long Lake. The fish were caught so that he could dissect them and discover what they had eaten. Moyle netted fish at different times of the day and at midnight. He wanted to find out whether the feeding activity or the food of minnows changed over the course of a day.

Peter Moyle also wanted to find out how the minnows were distributed in the lake. So he joined the fish underwater, swimming with scuba gear. He did this at various times of the day and, using special lights, after dark too. The fish were not disturbed by his presence and went about their normal lives.

Immediately after these underwater explorations Moyle made notes about what he had seen. The notes included facts like these: 1) time of day 2) weather 3) depth of water 4) kinds of fish seen 5) position of fish in the water and 6) whether the bot-

tom was bare, covered with rocks, or with plants.

The minnows of Long Lake spent most of their lives close together in shallow waters. At first glance it seemed that they must compete directly for both food and space. However, Peter Moyle's painstaking work revealed how the niches of the minnows varied.

One member of the minnow family, the mimic shiner, was the most abundant fish in the lake. Large schools of these shiners swam in the shallows. (In late summer, during their breeding season, one school was made up of at least 15,000 shiners.) In the early morning mimic shiners fed in the middle zone of the water, where little crustaceans known as *Daphnia* were plentiful. During the day the shiners fed near the surface or near the bottom, but not in midwater.

Schools of shiners swam back and forth along the lakeshore as they fed. Toward evening these schools broke up into groups of ten to fifteen fish. Most of these small groups swam out into deeper water. When Peter Moyle explored underwater at night, he found the mimic shiners lying on the bottom.

The second most common fish of Long Lake was the bluntnose minnow. This species fed mostly on the bottom and especially in open areas among beds of plants. It ate insects, algae, and other foods it found near or on the bottom. Its feeding habits changed very little during the day. At night bluntnose minnows rested on the bottom too.

In water about two meters (six and a half feet) deep, Moyle found many small, independent schools of bluntnose minnows. In shallower water (less than one meter deep), he discovered that small schools

---

above: mimic shiners
below: bluntnose minnow feeding
Most minnows and shiners are three to five inches long.

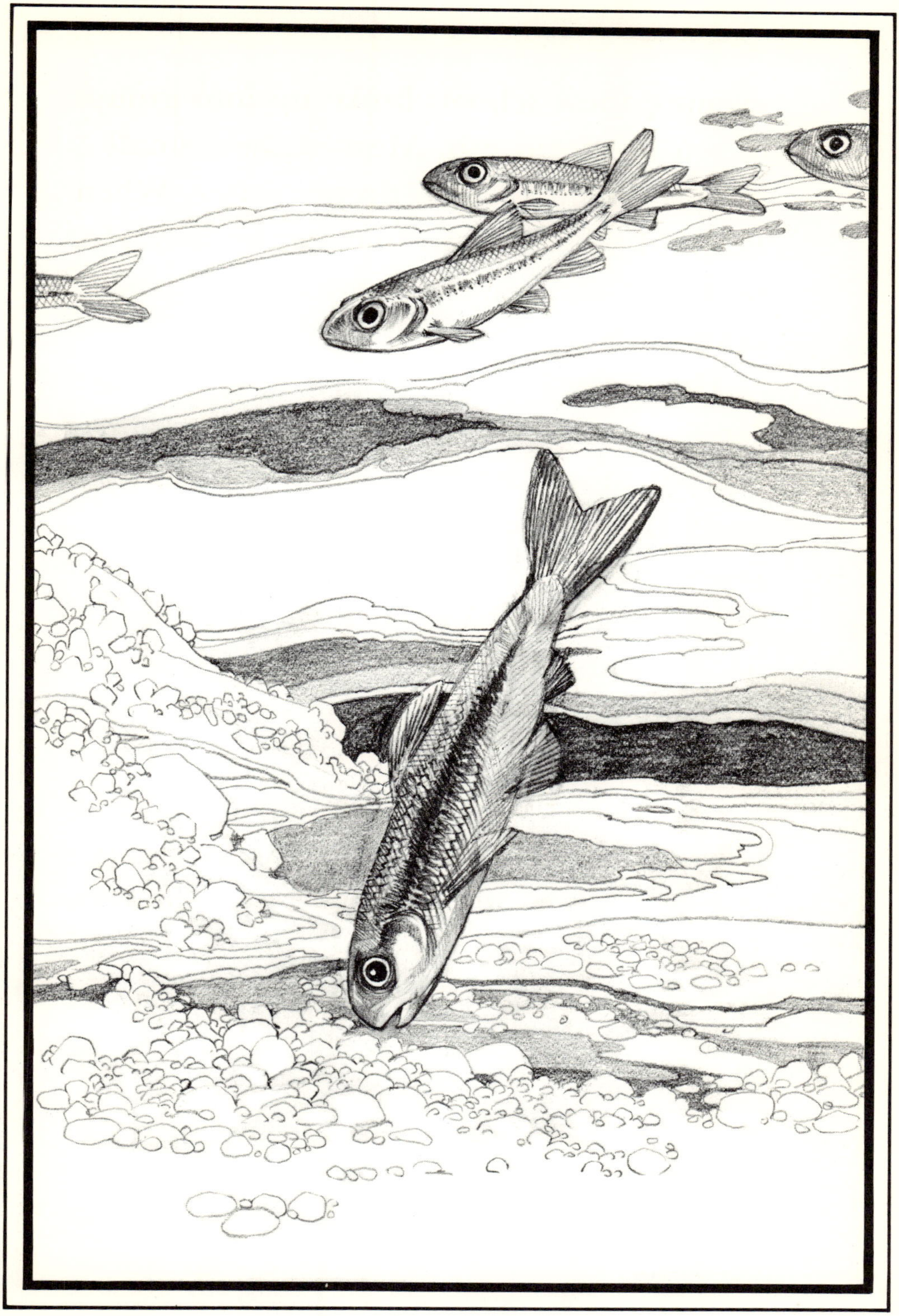

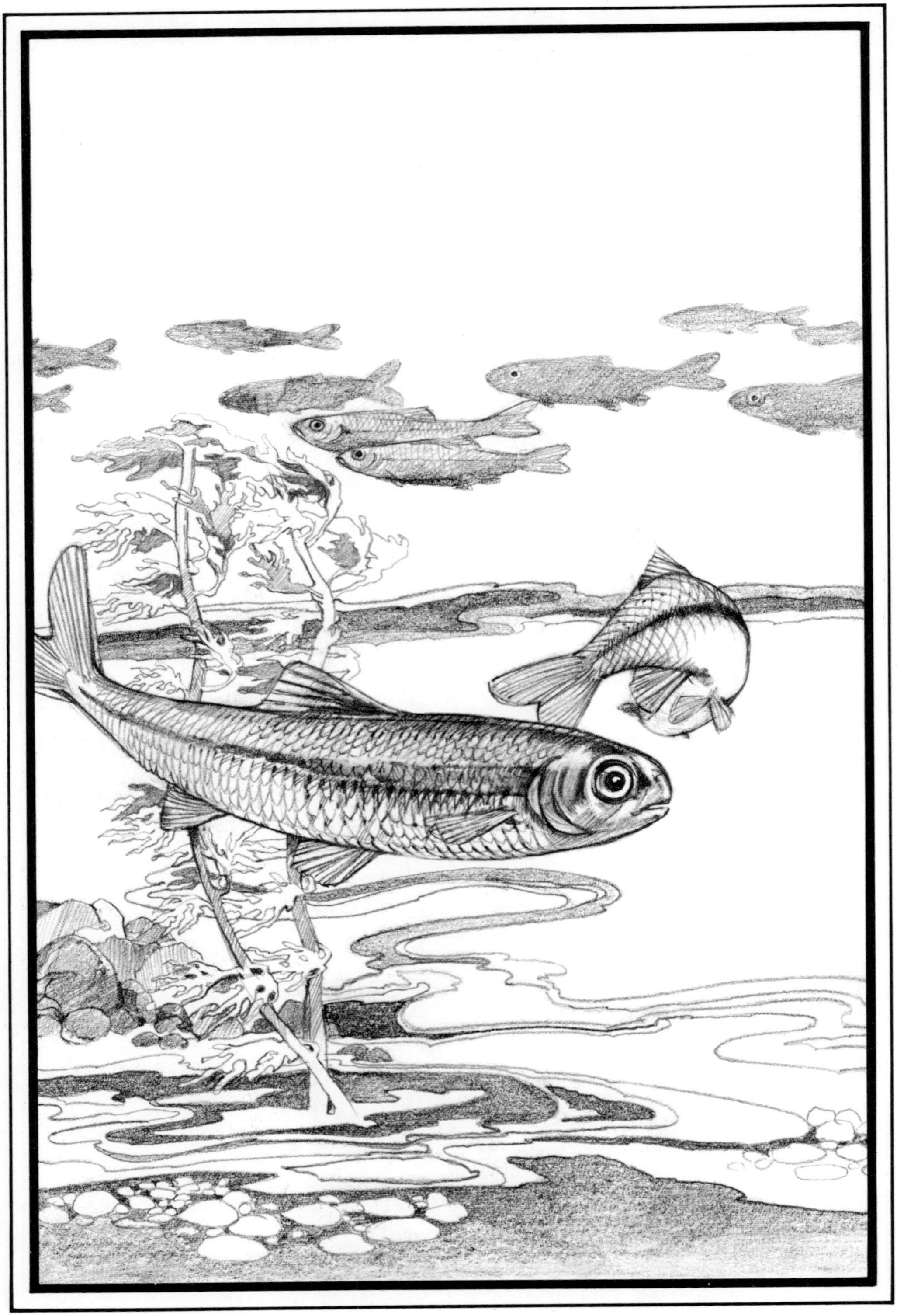

of bluntnose minnows swam just behind large schools of mimic shiners. These minnows seemed to be smaller than average. They were probably young fish. Moyle suspected that the minnows stayed near the shiner schools because they offered protection. (Schooling helps protect fish from predatory animals that try to eat them.)

The third member of the minnow family in Long Lake was the common shiner. Its population in the lake varied more than that of mimic shiners or bluntnose minnows. Moyle found that common shiners were opportunistic feeders. That is, they fed wherever food was most plentiful, regardless of the time of day—on the bottom, among plants, in midwater, or at the surface.

The smallest common shiners were usually found in shallow water. They stayed

---

bluntnose minnows (below)
near a school of common shiners (above)

on the outer edges of the big schools of mimic shiners or actually mixed in with these schools. Older, larger common shiners formed small schools in deeper water, swimming a bit above dense growths of plants.

The minnows of Long Lake certainly differed in their preferred feeding areas. Most of the time they fed in different places on different kinds of food. One morning, however, Peter Moyle found that both mimic shiners and bluntnose minnows had gorged themselves on midges. Great numbers of these little insects had been emerging at the water's surface in the morning. That evening, however, the bluntnose minnows fed near the bottom as usual, and the mimic shiners fed near the surface.

Also keeping the three kinds of minnows apart was a difference in their breeding times and breeding places. As a result, the young of one species did not compete for food with other kinds. This was another important difference in the niches of these fishes.

Peter Moyle and other biologists caught a few individuals of other minnow species in Long Lake. They were probably introduced accidentally by fishermen, who often use minnows as bait to catch bigger fish. Most of these minnows were those that normally live in streams or bogs. Therefore, they had little chance of establishing populations in the habitat of Long Lake.

Some of the other minnow species normally lived in lakes and ponds, however, and their chances were better. Still, their numbers remained small. Why? Competition with the well-established minnow species is certainly one answer. Two of the species brought to the lake by fishermen were shiners that appear to have niches similar to those of mimic shiners and so would compete with them. Another species was the fathead minnow. It normally lives in ways very much like those of the bluntnose minnow and so would have to compete with it for food and space.

From his study Peter Moyle concluded that the three common species in Long Lake competed very little with each other. Furthermore, their niches also probably kept similar kinds of minnows from becoming established in the lake.

Desert Rodents

While Peter Moyle swam among minnows in Minnesota, other biologists were studying animal niches in a very different environment—the Sonoran Desert in Arizona. The animals studied were seed-eating rodents, which are abundant and varied in deserts. Hundreds of individuals may live on only an acre of land. Often several kinds are closely related and have similar ways of life. For example, on one acre of land in Arizona, six species of pocket mice or kangaroo rats may emerge from underground burrows at night, gather seeds and stuff them into fur-lined cheek pouches, then carry the seeds back to their burrows.

Several biologists have studied rodents in the Southwest in order to find out more about their niches. During the 1960s some detailed studies were made of the rodents and plants on twenty-six large, circular plots of desert land in Arizona. The biologists took a census of each plot by catching rodents in traps baited with seeds. They wanted to see whether rodent populations were affected by the distribution of plant life.

They also studied the soils of the plots to determine whether differences in soil might affect the burrowing rodents. In Colorado, the distribution of four species of pocket gophers depends very much on the depth and texture of the soil in different places. In Arizona, however, the effect of desert soils on burrowing rodents was less clear. One large species, the bannertail kangaroo rat, seemed to need firm soil in

---

bannertail kangaroo rat,
about twelve to fifteen inches long including its tail

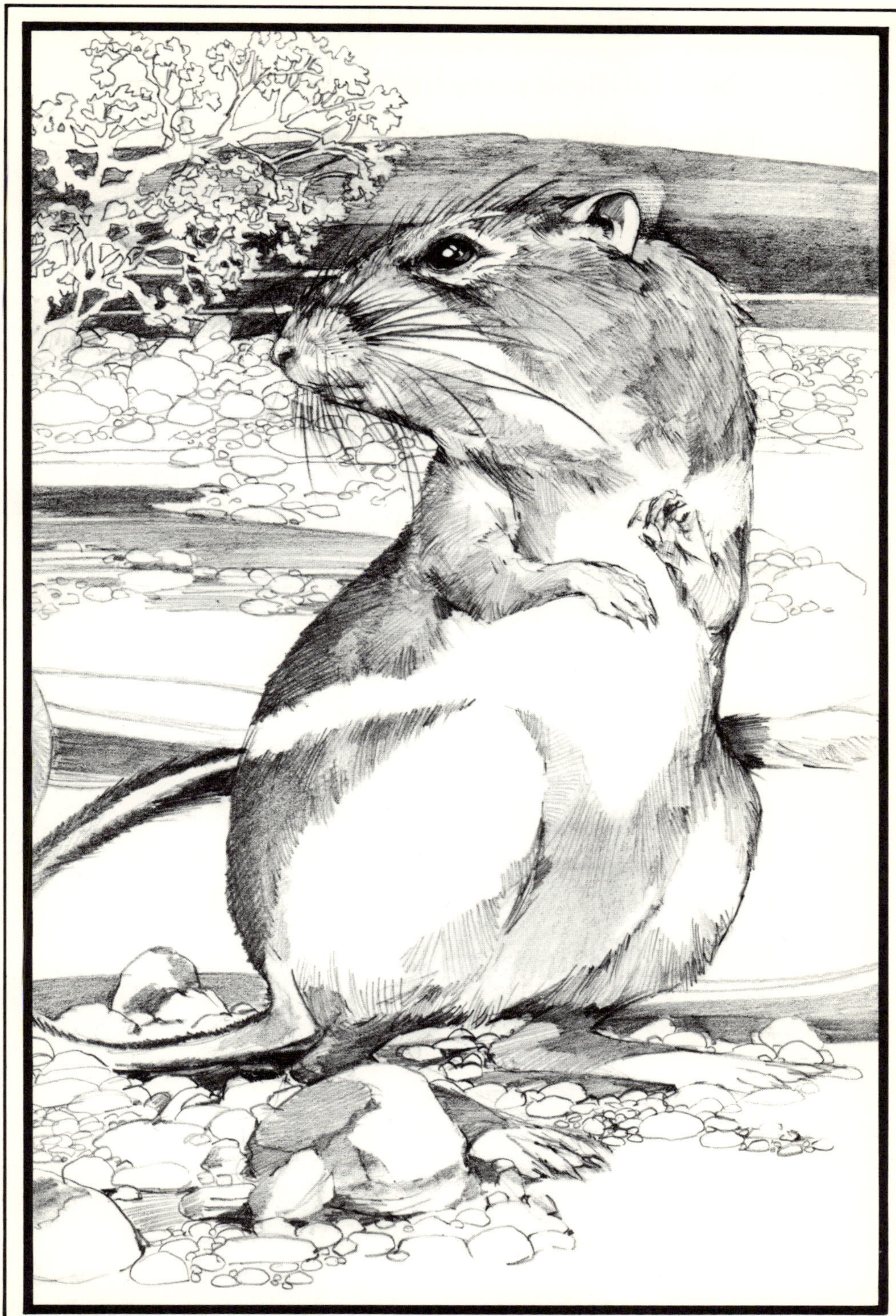

which to dig its big tunnels. One of the smallest species, the Arizona pocket mouse, was not caught on firm soil. Perhaps it had difficulty digging burrows in such soil.

The importance of plants in the rodents' niches was clearer. The biologists caught the silky pocket mouse in low, dense grasses. A larger species, the hispid pocket mouse, was found in taller grasses. The biologists called several species "bush mice," because they all seemed to need a habitat of bushy growth.

Among the bush mice, the Bailey pocket mouse was captured on every plot where a plant named jojoba (pronounced ho-HO-ba) grew. (Jojoba bears small, leathery leaves and brown, oily seeds.) When jojoba plants were absent, no Bailey pocket mice were caught. Its niche was

---

above: silky pocket mouse,
about four to five inches long including its tail
below: hispid pocket mouse,
about eight to ten inches long including its tail

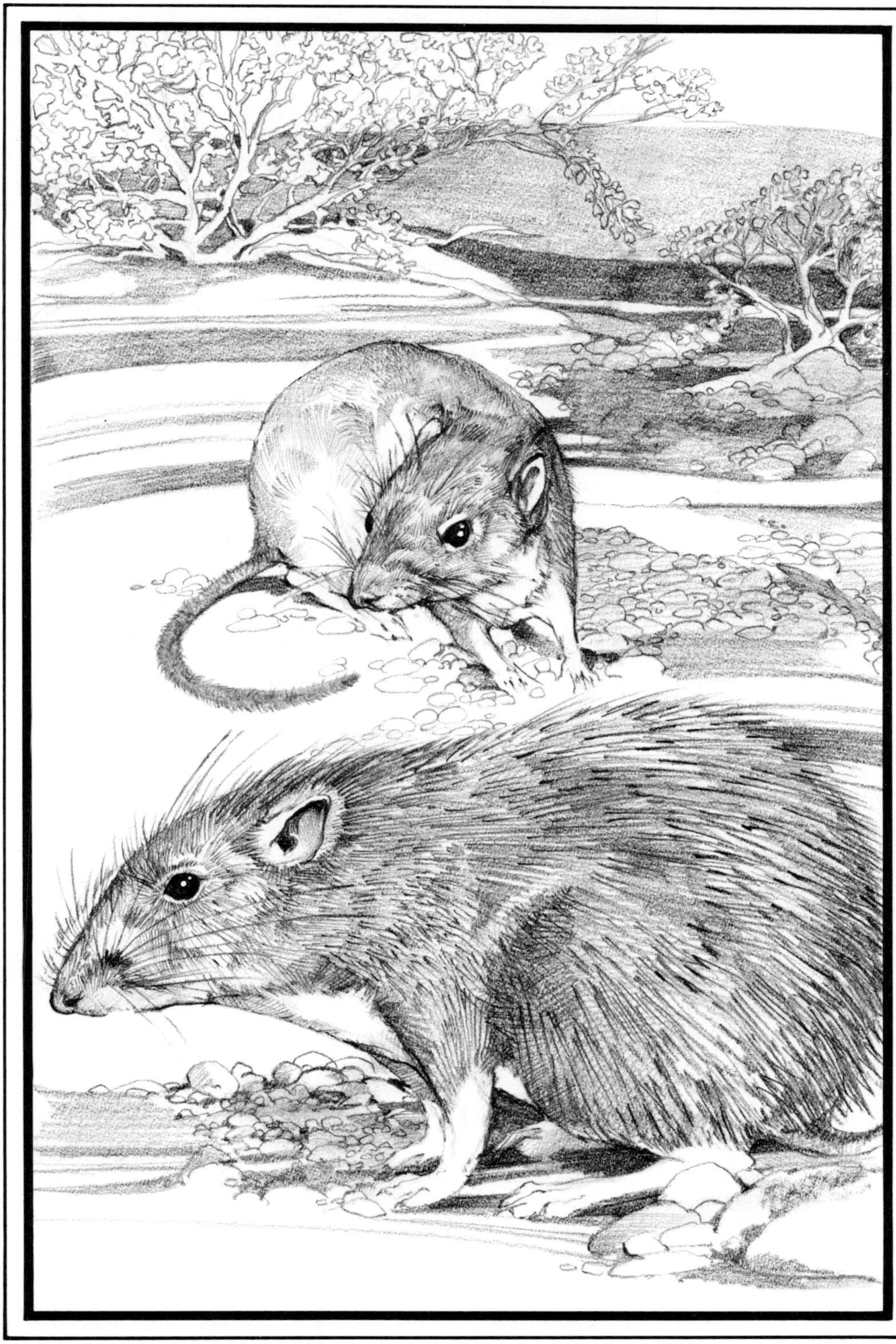

often filled by another, slightly smaller rodent, the desert pocket mouse.

The niches of the other bush mice also seemed to differ. One species seemed to prefer dense bushes; another preferred bushes with more open foliage. There wasn't enough information to determine exactly how the niches of all of the seed-eating rodents differed. But this study did give some ideas about how several kinds of rodents could live close together and share the resources of their community.

A few years later, in the early 1970s, two biologists discovered more about the niches of rodents in desert communities. This time the study areas were eighteen large sand dunes in Nevada, California, and Utah. James Brown and Gerald Lieberman set traps out in the open and also near and beneath shrubs that grew on the dunes. They used snap traps that killed the rodents. In this way they were able to collect and study seeds from the cheek pouches of six different species.

They discovered that each species ate a wide range of different-sized seeds. In general, however, the smallest rodents ate the smallest seeds, and the bigger rodents ate bigger seeds. Thus, two species of similar size would compete for the same food.

But the trapping results showed that such direct competition was usually avoided. Species of the same size were not common on the same dune. For example, if one of the smallest species, the little pocket mouse, was common on a dune, another small rodent, the Western harvest mouse, was scarce. Apparently even an animal's size can be a vital part of its niche.

The study also revealed some important information about the degree of similarity, or overlap, among species in their use of a resource. The two biologists discovered, for example, overlap in the sizes of seeds gathered by the rodents. At least four fifths of one rodent's food was also poten-

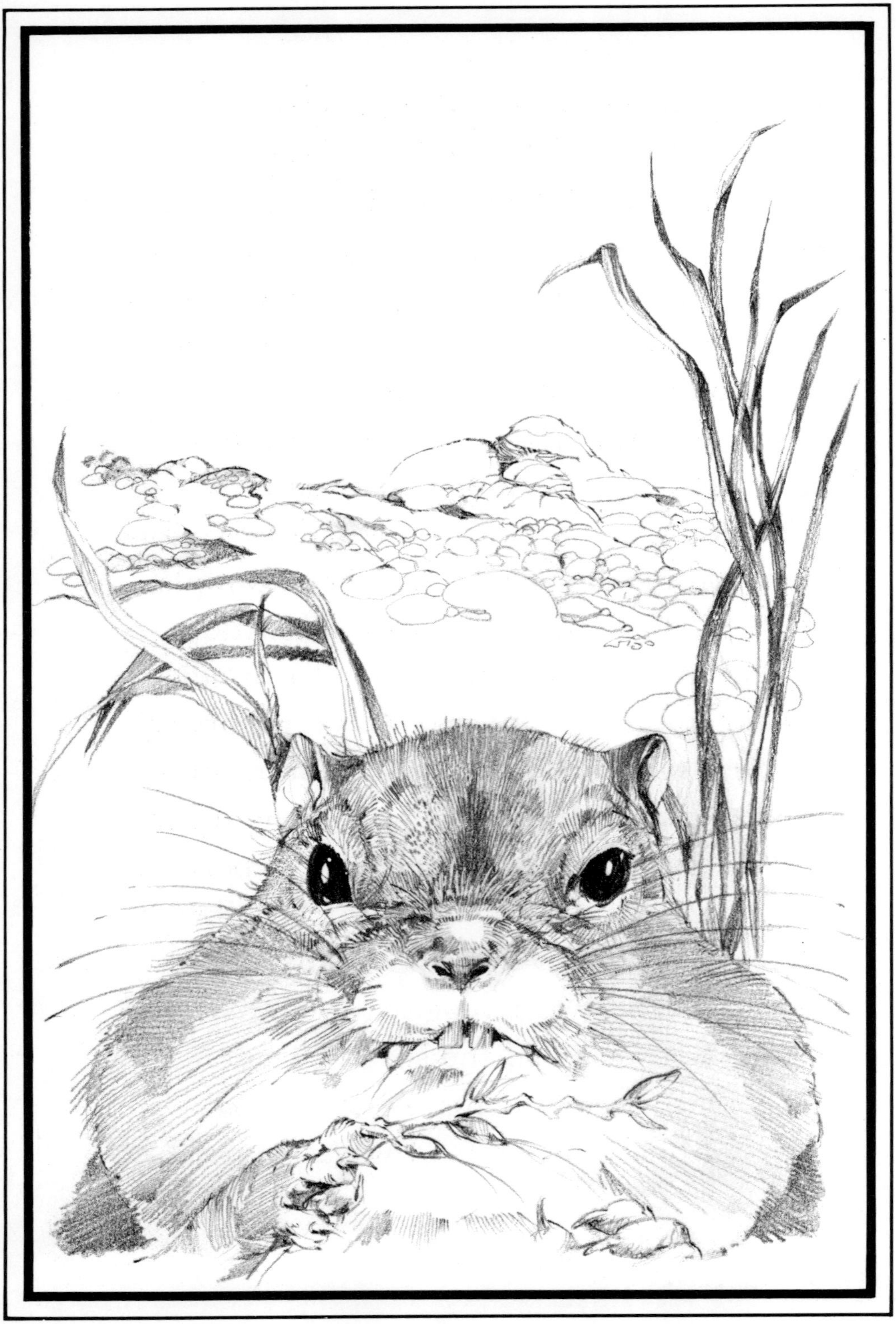

tial food for other species. Only a fifth or less of a rodent's food seemed free of competition from other rodents. This amount was a small advantage, but it was often enough to enable species to coexist.

It was often not enough, however, when food was scarce. Brown and Lieberman caught only a few species of rodents on dunes where plants produced small or undependable crops of seeds. They caught the greatest variety of rodents on dunes that had the most food. More species could coexist on such dunes, because there was less competition for the plentiful seeds.

This study is significant because it was one of the first to define the amount of overlap between the niches of different species. It also showed that species can have very similar needs and still coexist, at least in communities where resources are not scarce.

Kangaroo rats and pocket mice collect food in their fur-lined cheek pouches.

Understanding Niches

When George Schaller spent three years at Serengeti National Park in Tanzania, his goal was to study the African lion. In the course of his investigation, however, he also made many observations of that community's five large predators. He learned something about their niches. The predators usually hunted at different times of the day and lived in different habitats. Lions were mainly found in wooded areas; cheetahs and hyenas in the plains and the borders between plains and woods. Leopards lived in thickets and forests near riv-

---

Cheetahs and hyenas often share the same habitat, but hunt at different times.

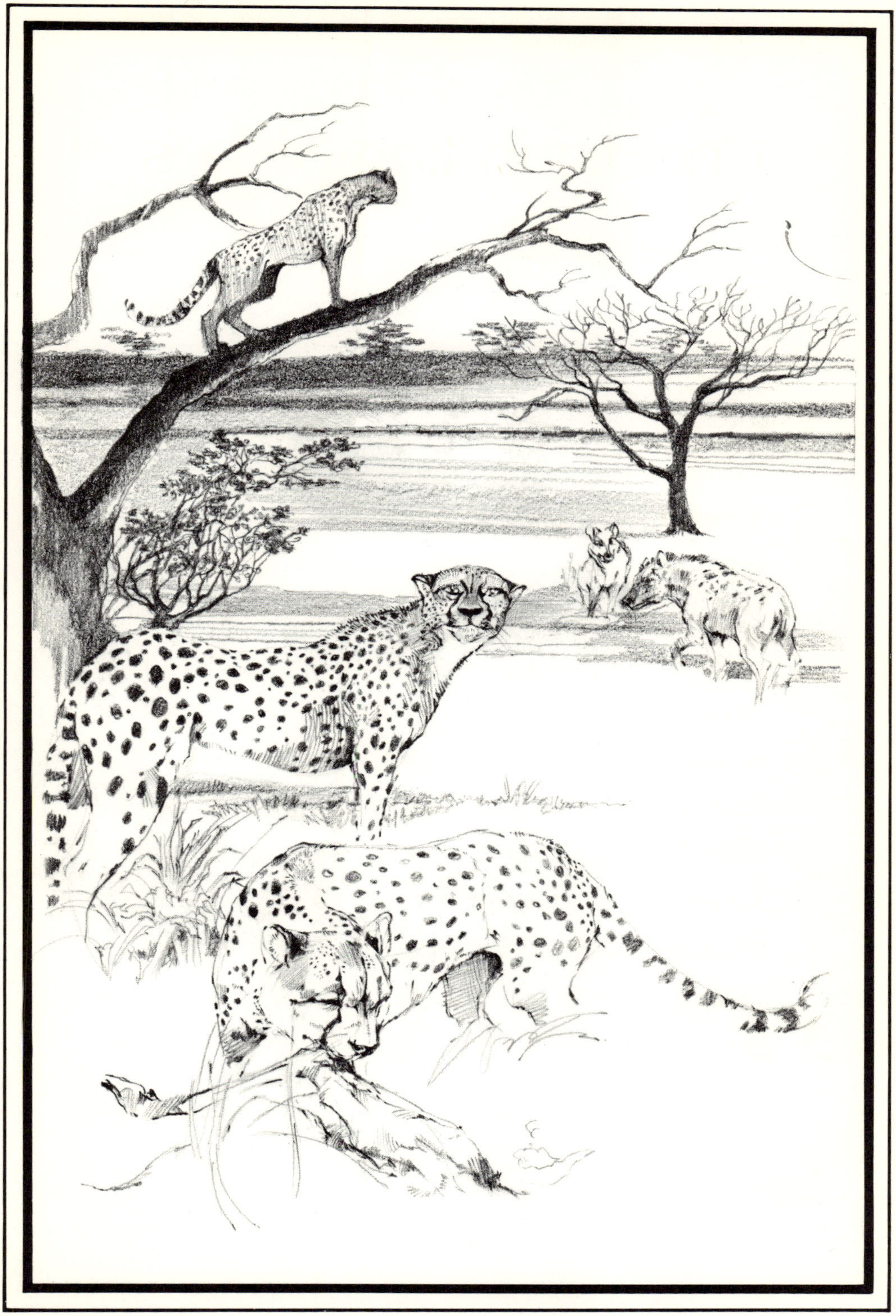

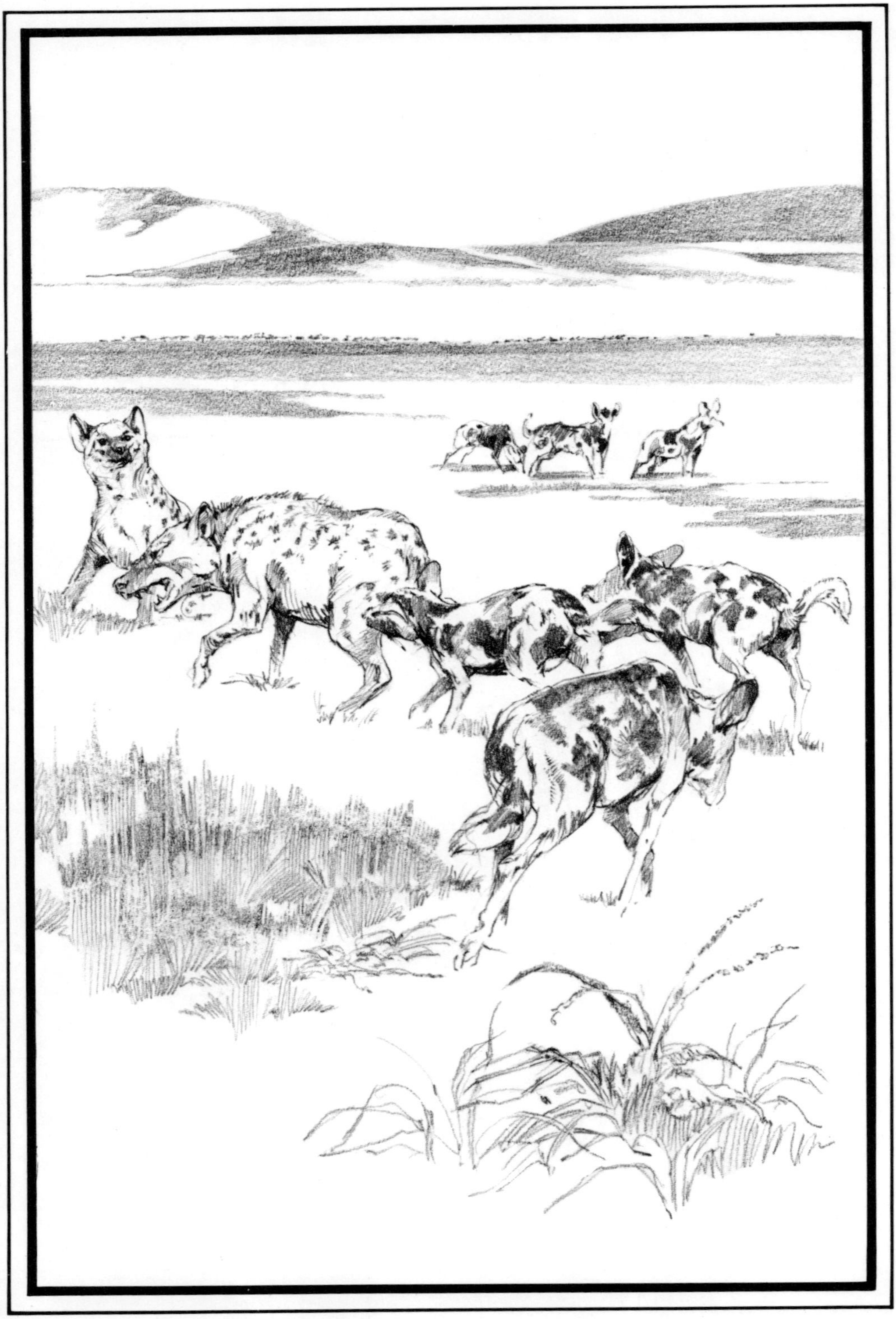

ers, African wild dogs in both woods and plains about equally.

Even though Schaller's study focused mainly on one species, he added to the understanding of animal niches in general. From sources like his work and from other more direct studies, scientists have gained a lot of information about resource partitioning.

In 1974, Thomas Schoener, a biologist at Harvard University, analyzed the results of eighty-one studies of coexisting species. In 90 percent of the cases the species were separated by differences in habitat. In 78 percent of the cases they were separated by differences in food, and in 41 percent by differences in times of activity. Of course, the niches of many species included differences in both habitat and food and sometimes in all three factors.

According to Schoener's study, different

hyenas (on the left) and wild dogs in Africa

times of activity were especially common among coexisting populations of predators—including the ones that George Schaller observed in Africa. The reason was probably because the animal prey of predators have different peaks of activity. In contrast, the food of plant eaters is usually available around the clock. So coexisting populations of plant eaters are more likely to have niches that differ in kinds of food or habitat, rather than in time of activity.

If this explanation is correct, biologists have gained a better understanding of predatory animals and of all nature. They also know more about the question of how animals coexist in communities. This question has led to dozens of studies during the last several decades. It will lead to many more because of the fascination and

The food of such plant eaters as mice, geese, and pronghorn antelopes (pictured) is available both day and night.

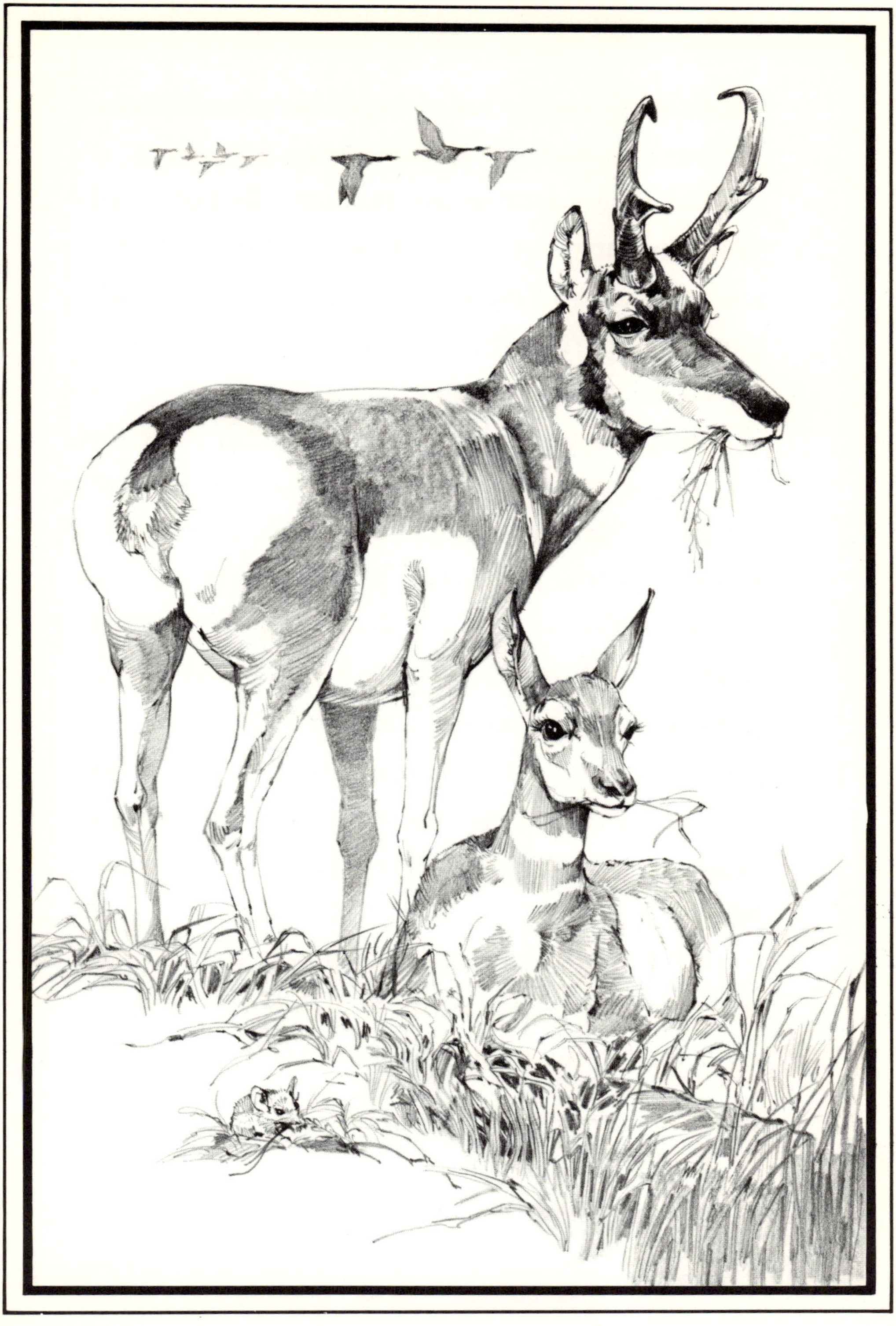

usefulness in discovering how grasshoppers or bats or hermit crabs share resources.

But other questions remain. It is important to sum up what all of the studies of niches have revealed so far. It is also important to recognize what they have *not* revealed.

There is plenty of evidence that animals have different niches in their communities. There is no proof, however, that the different niches are directly caused by competition for resources. To set up an experiment to prove or disprove this idea is probably impossible. Besides, there are more important questions to ask—not just *how* are animal niches arranged in a community but *why* are they arranged that way?

There are other forces at work in communities besides competition. One is predation. Some animal populations may be

---

Predation may have a powerful influence on some animal niches.

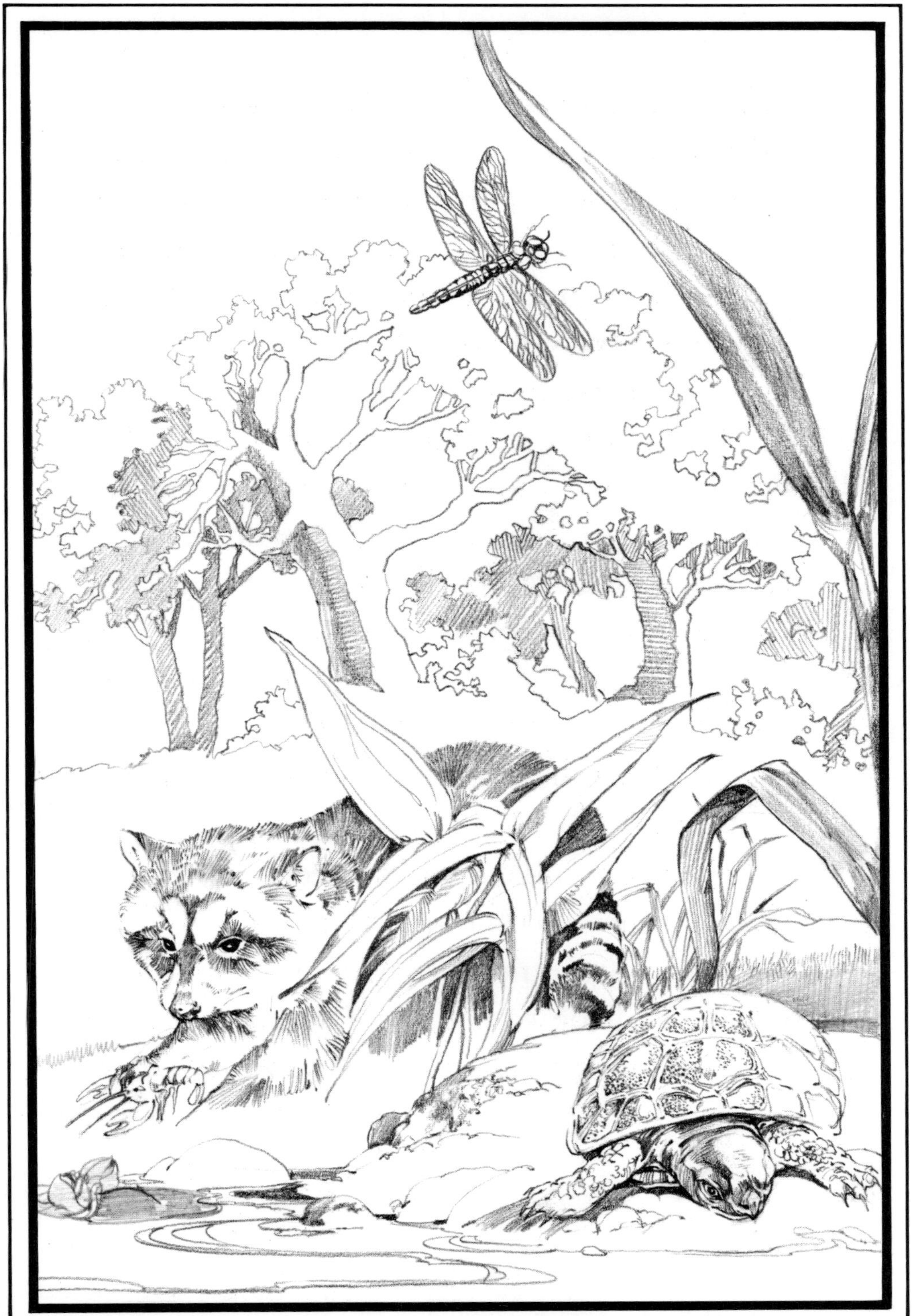

influenced by predators that try to eat them. Why does an animal feed at a certain time of day in a certain habitat? To avoid being eaten, to reduce competition, or both? Some biologists are trying to disentangle the effects of competition and predation on animal niches.

The understanding of animals and their roles in communities has grown a lot since the early experiments with beetles and parameciums. Scientists know much more about the lives of garter snakes, warblers, minnows, pocket mice, and other creatures. They have discovered how closely animals are tied to one another in their communities.

Scientists have also learned how complex nature is. One question leads to another, and another. Animals and their niches will be something for many to wonder about and to study for years to come.

Glossary

Biologist—a scientist who studies living things. Biologists often concentrate on a particular kind of life and are named for this interest, for example, plants (botanist), insects (entomologist), reptiles (herpetologist).

Community—all of the populations occurring in a particular area, for example, the plant and animal populations in a city park or a backyard.

Competition—a striving or vying with others for food or some other necessity of life. Although competition has effects on entire species and populations of animals and plants, it is experienced by individuals, for example, by two birds. This book is about competition among different species (interspecific); there is also intraspecific competition within the same species.

Crustaceans—members of the class Crustacea, which include crayfish, lobsters, crabs, shrimp, copepods, and sow bugs. All have a hard outer skeleton, segmented bodies, and paired, jointed legs.

Ecology—the science that examines the relationships between living things and their environment.

Environment—all of the surroundings of an organism,

including other living things, climate, and soils.
Habitat—the kind of community in which an organism lives. For example, the habitat of the mimic shiner is usually a lake.
Niche—the role an organism, population, or species plays; its "occupation" in its community, including all of the effects it has on other life and its response to nonliving things. An exact definition of this term is still debated by ecologists.
Ornithologist—a scientist who studies birds.
Population—the number of individuals of a certain kind that live in a certain area at a certain time. For example, the human population of the earth was four billion in 1975.
Predators—animals that kill other animals for food. They include sharks, foxes, warblers, ladybugs, and humans.
Resource partitioning—the ways in which a community's animal species coexist by sharing such resources as food and space. Also called "ecological segregation."
Rodents—members of the mammalian class Rodentia, which include squirrels, mice, rats, lemmings, beavers, and gophers (but not rabbits and hares). They are gnawing mammals, with four prominent yellow or orange teeth, which continue to grow throughout a rodent's entire life.
Species—a population or many populations of an organism that have characteristics in common, which make them different from individuals of other species populations. The members of a species share a common and unique inheritance. (Members of a species interbreed with each other but not with members of other species.)

Further Reading

The scientific journals listed here may be found in some public libraries, or in university and natural-history-museum libraries.

Brown, James, and Lieberman, Gerald, "Resource Utilization and Coexistence of Seed-eating Desert Rodents in Sand Dune Habitats." *Ecology,* Vol. 54, No. 4 (1973), pp. 788–797.

Carpenter, Charles, "Comparative Ecology of the Common Garter Snake, the Ribbon Snake, and Butler's Garter Snake in Mixed Populations." *Ecological Monographs,* Vol. 22, No. 4 (1952), pp. 235–258.

Gause, B.F., *The Struggle for Existence.* Baltimore: Williams and Wilkins, 1934 (also available in paperback from Dover Publications, New York, 1971).

Hardin, Garrett, "The Competitive Exclusion Principle." *Science,* 29 April 1960, pp. 1292–1297.

Kormondy, Edward, *Concepts of Ecology.* Englewood Cliffs, New Jersey: Prentice-Hall, Inc., 1969.

MacArthur, Robert, "Population Ecology of Some Warblers of Northeastern Coniferous Forests." *Ecology,* Vol. 39, No. 4 (1958), pp. 599–619.

Makarewicz, Joseph, and Likens, Gene, "Niche Analysis of a Zooplankton Community." *Science,* 5 December 1975, pp. 1000–1003.

Miller, Richard, "Ecology and Distribution of Pocket Gophers (Geomyidae) in Colorado." *Ecology,* Vol. 45, No. 2 (1964), pp. 256–272.

Moyle, Peter, "Ecological Segregation Among Three Species of Minnows (Cyprinidae) in a Minnesota Lake." *Transactions of the American Fisheries Society,* Vol. 102, No. 4 (1973), pp. 794–805.

Pringle, Laurence, *Ecology: Science of Survival.* New York: Macmillan Publishing Company, 1971.

Rosenzweig, Michael, and Winakur, Jerald, "Population Ecology of Desert Rodent Communities: Habitats and Environmental Complexity." *Ecology,* Vol. 50, No. 4 (1969), pp. 558–572.

Schaller, George, *The Serengeti Lion.* Chicago: The University of Chicago Press, 1972.

Schoener, Thomas, "Resource Partitioning in Ecological Communities." *Science,* 5 July 1974, pp. 27–39.

Smith, Robert Leo, *Ecology and Field Biology.* New York: Harper & Row, 1966.

Whittaker, R.H., Levin, S.A., and Root, R.B., "Niche, Habitat, and Ecotope." *The American Naturalist,* Vol. 107, No. 955 (1973), pp. 321–338.

Index
*indicates illustration

African lion, 50
African wild dog, 52*, 53
Arizona pocket mouse, 44
Bailey pocket mouse, 44
Bay-breasted warbler, 24–25, 26*
Birds, 5, 10, 15, 18; *see also* individual species
Blackburnian warbler, 23*, 24, 27
Black-throated green warbler, 24, 28*
Bluntnose minnows, 34, 35*, 36*, 37, 38, 40
Brown, James, 46, 49
Bush mice, 44, 46
Butler's garter snake, 15, 17–18
Cape May warbler, 23*, 24
Carpenter, Charles, 15, 17, 18, 21, 22
Cheetahs, 50, 51*
Common garter snake, 15, 16*, 18

Common shiners, 36*, 37–38
Communities, 6, 8, 10, 11, 14, 15, 46, 49, 50, 54, 56, 58
Competition, 10, 13–14, 38, 39–40, 47, 49, 56, 58
Crombie, A.C., 13
Daphnia, 33
Darwin, Charles, 10
Desert pocket mouse, 46
Evolution, 14
Fathead minnows, 40
Feeding zones, of minnows, 33, 34, 37, 38; of warblers, 23*, 24–25, 26*, 27, 29
Food, as a resource, 6, 10, 11, 14, 21, 54; *see also* niche
Frogs, 18, 19*
Gause, B.F., 11
Grain beetles, 12*, 13, 58
Grinnell, Joseph, 10
Habitat, differences among species, 11, 13, 18, 21, 33–34, 37–38, 39, 50, 53, 54, 58

63

Hispid pocket mouse, 44, 45*
Hyenas, 50, 51*, 52*
Insects, 5, 10, 15, 18, 22, 24, 27, 34, 38
Jojoba, 44
Kangaroo rats, 41, 42, 43*
Leopards, 50
Lieberman, Gerald, 46, 49
Little pocket mouse, 47
Long Lake (Minnesota), 30–40
MacArthur, Robert, 22, 24, 25, 27, 29
Mice, 8, 9*, 18, 55*; *see also* pocket mice, individual species
Mimic shiners, 33–34, 35*, 37, 38, 39
Moyle, Peter, 30–31, 33–34, 37–40, 41
Myrtle warbler, 25, 26*
Niche, defined, 6, 8; of African predators, 50, 53; of desert rodents, 41, 42, 44, 46, 47, 49; of garter snakes, 17–21; of mice, 8; of minnows, 30, 33–34, 37–40; of parameciums, 11, 13; of warblers, 24–25, 27, 29
Numbers, of animal species, 5
Overlap, of animal niches, 29, 47, 49
Owl, 8, 9*

Parameciums, 11, 58
Pocket gophers, 42
Pocket mice, 41, 44, 45*, 46, 47, 58; *see also* individual species
Populations, 6, 8, 10, 21, 31, 42, 54
Predators, 37, 50, 53, 54
Predation, effect on niches, 56, 58
Pronghorn antelope, 55*
Resources, 6, 10, 11, 13, 14, 22, 30, 46, 47, 49; *see also* food, niche
Resource partitioning, 30, 53
Ribbon snake, 15, 18, 19*, 20*
Rodents, 41, 42, 46, 47, 49; *see also* mice, pocket mice
Schaller, George, 50, 53, 54
Schoener, Thomas, 53
Schooling of fish, 37
Serengeti National Park (Africa), 50
Silky pocket mouse, 44, 45*
Soil, effects on burrowing rodents, 42, 44
Sonoran Desert, 41
Time, of animal activity, 14, 27, 29, 31, 37, 50, 53, 54, 58
Warblers, 22, 24, 58; *see also* individual species
Western harvest mouse, 47